Valentine's Day Crafts

by Claire Mathiowetz • illustrated by Mernie Gallagher-Cole

The Child's World®
childsworld.com

Published by The Child's World®
1980 Lookout Drive • Mankato, MN 56003-1705
800-599-READ • www.childsworld.com

Acknowledgments
The Child's World®: Mary Swensen, Publishing Director
Red Line Editorial: Editorial direction and production
The Design Lab: Design

Photographs ©: iStockphoto, 4

ISBN 9781503808225
LCCN 2015958200

Printed in the United States of America
Mankato, MN
June, 2016
PA02298

About the Author
Claire Mathiowetz is an editor of children's books. She loves all holidays, but especially Valentine's Day because she shares it with her birthday. Claire lives in Minnesota and dreams of owning her own dog one day.

About the Illustrator
Mernie Gallagher-Cole is an artist living in West Chester, Pennsylvania. She has illustrated many books, games, and puzzles for children. She loves crafts and tries to be creative every day.

Table of Contents

Introduction to Valentine's Day

Valentine's Day began long, long ago. People first began to **celebrate** around 400 AD. But where did the holiday come from? No one knows for sure. Most people believe it is named after a priest. His name was Saint Valentine.

The story begins with a man named Claudius. He was the ruler of Rome in the 200s AD. Claudius stopped young men from getting married. He thought it would make

Valentine's Day is a great time to show your family how much you love them.

them better soldiers. But Saint Valentine disagreed. He wed people in secret. Then Claudius found out. He had Saint Valentine killed. Saint Valentine wrote a note to his love the night before he died. He signed it "From your Valentine." It is said he died on February 14.

Cupid is also a part of Valentine's Day. His story comes from Rome. Cupid is known as the god of love. He has wings. He also carries a bow and arrow. People fall in love when Cupid shoots them with his arrows.

February 14 officially became the day of love around the Middle Ages. People celebrate Valentine's Day in many ways. Some send flowers or chocolates to their loves. Others send cards to friends or family. Valentine's Day is not just about romance. It is meant to show people that you care about them.

Check out these fun crafts you can make this Valentine's Day. Give them to anyone close to your heart. Let's get started!

Construction Paper Lollipop Flowers

Many people give flowers for Valentine's Day. Roses are the most common flower to give. More than 200 million roses are grown for the holiday each year. Flowers are a nice way to show you care.

MATERIALS

- ☐ Card stock paper
- ☐ Pencil
- ☐ Ruler
- ☐ Scissors
- ☐ Construction paper
- ☐ Hole punch
- ☐ Glue
- ☐ Lollipops

STEPS

1. Take a sheet of card stock paper. Fold it in half the long way. Grab your pencil and your ruler. Mark 3 inches (7.6 cm) tall by 1.25 inches wide (3.8 cm) on the folded edge.

2. Along the fold, draw half of a heart. Follow the example. They show how tall and wide your heart should be. Cut out the heart using the scissors.

3. Pick a sheet of construction paper. It can be any color. Fold it in half the long way.

4. Take the card stock heart you just cut out. Do not unfold it. Use the pencil to trace it along the fold of the construction paper. Do this four times. Cut out the four hearts.

1.25"

3"

5. Unfold the four hearts. Lay them on top of each other. Make sure they line up exactly.

6. Mark .25 inches (.6 cm) from the bottom of the hearts. Use the hole punch to make a hole at the mark. Be sure the hole goes through all four hearts.

7. Put glue around the hole of each heart. Do not cover the hole with glue.

8. Place one heart on top of the next to form a circle. These will be the flower petals. Make sure all of the holes line up. Wait for the glue to dry.

9. Pick a lollipop. This will be the stem of your flower. Stick it through the hole. Now your flower is ready for your valentine!

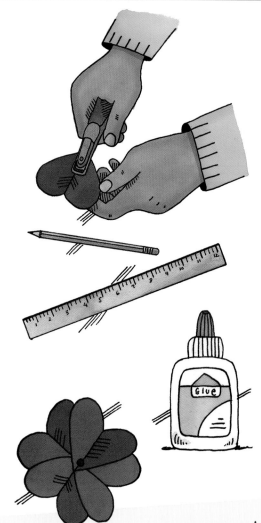

These flowers can be extra special. Add a message or a drawing to the petals. Your valentine will love the thought. These flowers will not die. That is the best part of the gift.

Smudge Valentines

The oldest known valentine gift is from 1477. But it was not common to send valentines until years later. Valentines became popular in England around the 1700s. The fad came to the United States in the mid-1800s. Today, more than 1 billion cards are sent on Valentine's Day.

MATERIALS

- [x] White paper
- [ ] Pencil
- [x] Scissors
- [x] Newspaper
- [x] Paint
- [x] Paintbrush
- [ ] Glue
- [x] Construction paper
- [x] Markers

STEPS

1. Take out a sheet of white paper. Fold it in half the long way. Use the pencil to draw half of a heart along the fold. Cover as much of the paper as possible. Use the scissors to cut out the heart.

2. Lay newspaper down on a flat surface. Unfold the heart.

3. Take out the paint and the paintbrush. Pick any paint colors you like. Paint on only half of the heart. Use the folded line in the middle as your guide. You can paint shapes or use other colors. Make sure the paint is thick.

4. Before the paint dries, fold the two sides of the heart together. Lightly press on the closed heart. Unfold the heart. The paint will have pressed onto the other side. Now you have a cool design! Let the paint dry.

5. Put glue on the back of the heart. Then place it on a sheet of construction paper. Cut the construction paper around the heart.

6. Add a **personal** message to the back of your valentine. Use a marker. Now it is ready to give to someone special!

This craft is perfect for those who like to get a little messy. You can make hearts with the paint. Or you could paint stripes, zigzags, or stars. You can also paint your name, or a friend's! There are tons of patterns you could paint. So roll up your sleeves and get creative!

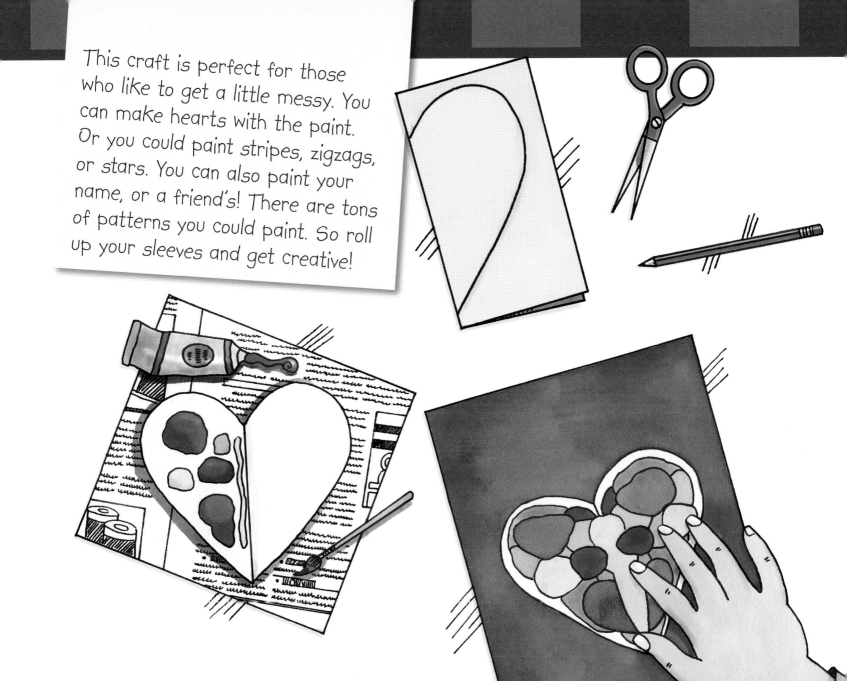

Watercolor Paper Hearts

Valentine's Day is celebrated around the world. But only six countries officially observe the holiday. Those countries are the United States, Canada, Mexico, France, the United Kingdom, and Australia. This Valentine's Day, make these colorful hearts as a gift. They will brighten anyone's day!

MATERIALS

- [ ] Scissors
- [ ] Tissue paper
- [ ] Card stock paper
- [ ] Paintbrush
- [ ] Water

STEPS

1. Use the scissors to cut out at least 20 strips of tissue paper. They can be any size and color.
2. Take a sheet of card stock paper. Cut out a heart of any size.

3. Take a tissue paper strip. Lay it on top of the heart. Using the paintbrush, put water over the tissue paper. This helps it stick to the heart.

4. **Repeat** step 3 until the heart is covered. The strips will overlap.

5. Let the tissue paper soak into the heart. Set it aside for ten minutes.

6. Peel the wet tissue paper off of the heart. Then let the heart dry. You now have an awesome watercolor valentine!

These hearts can easily be added to a card. Just tape them onto construction paper. Fold the paper in half. Then, add a thoughtful message. Now you have a nice homemade card for Valentine's Day!

Do-It-Yourself Valentine Mailbox

Giving valentines can be so much fun. But it is also fun to get valentines. This mailbox is a great place to store your treats.

MATERIALS

- ☐ Glue
- ☐ Cereal box
- ☐ Scissors
- ☐ Ruler
- ☐ Construction paper
- ☐ Markers

STEPS

1. Glue the top of a cereal box shut. Wait for the glue to dry.

2. Use the scissors to cut the short edge of the top of the box. Then keep cutting. Measure and cut 4 inches (10 cm) down the front of the cereal box. Cut straight across the front of the box. Then cut toward the top of the box. Cut the other short side. This should all be one smooth cut. The box should now have a flap.

3. Lift up the flap. Inside of the box are two small tabs. Cut them off.

4. Turn your box so the top is facing up. Cut an opening in the middle of the top. Make it 5 inches (12.7 cm) long by 1 inch (2.5 cm) wide. This will be the opening for adding valentines.

5. Now it is time to **decorate** your mailbox. Use construction paper or markers. Leave your mailbox on your desk or in your room when you are finished. Friends or family can put valentines inside.

Mailboxes can also be made out of shoeboxes or tissue boxes. Ribbon, glitter, or buttons are other decorations you can use. Or add the word MAIL to the front of the box. This will make it look like a real mailbox.

Sweetheart Suncatchers

This craft is great for the cloudy winter. Watch the sun shine through your suncatcher. It will light up the room with fun colors.

MATERIALS

- ☑ Tissue paper
- ☐ Scissors
- ☑ Wax paper
- ☑ Liquid starch
- ☑ Paintbrush
- ☐ Double-sided tape

STEPS

1. Pick out different colors of tissue paper. Cut the tissue into small pieces using scissors. The pieces do not need to be the same sizes. The more shapes the better.

2. Lay the wax paper on a flat surface. Paint liquid starch onto the wax paper. Cover the whole paper or just a small area. This will be the size of your suncatcher.

3. Grab a handful of tissue paper pieces. Lay them on top of the wet wax paper. Be sure to overlap pieces. Use as many colors as possible.

4. Use the paintbrush to put liquid starch onto the tissue pieces. Make sure all the tissues are covered. Let the tissue paper dry.

5. Carefully peel the wax paper away from the tissue paper. Cut your suncatcher into the shape of a heart.

6. Add double-sided tape to the back of the heart. Place on a window. Watch as different colors fill the room.

Valentine Snow Globes

This craft will last long after the holiday is over. You will love how these look when they are finished. It is fun to see the pipe cleaners move in the water. It is also pretty when the glitter falls! These snow globes make an awesome gift for your valentine.

MATERIALS

- [ ] Any size glass jar with lid
- [ ] Thin brick size floral foam
- [ ] Craft glue
- [ ] Pipe cleaners
- [ ] Water
- [ ] Tablespoon
- [ ] Glitter

STEPS

1. Remove the lid from the glass jar. Cut the floral foam so it fits inside the lid.

You could also make X's and O's out of your pipe cleaners. X stands for kisses. O stands for hugs. It is common to sign cards using XOXO.

2. Apply craft glue to one side of the foam. Stick the glued side to the inside of the lid. Let it dry.

3. Make hearts using the pipe cleaners. Keep one end of the pipe cleaner straight. The straight end will stick into the foam. Make as many hearts as you want. You may need to cut the pipe cleaners to fit in the jar.

4. Stick the pipe cleaners into the floral foam when they are ready.

5. Fill the jar with water. Add 2 tablespoons of glitter. Then put the lid back on tightly.

6. Turn your snow globe upside down. Shake! Watch as the glitter swirls around the jar.

Glossary

celebrate (SEL-uh-brate) Celebrate means to do something special for an event. On Valentine's Day, people celebrate love.

decorate (DEK-uh-rate) Decorate means to add pretty things to something. The teacher wanted to decorate the room for Valentine's Day.

personal (PUR-suh-nuhl) Personal means belonging to a specific person. She made her grandma a personal card for Valentine's Day.

repeat (ri-PEET) Repeat means to do again. The directions said to repeat a step.

To Learn More

IN THE LIBRARY

Farmer, Jacqueline. *Valentine Be Mine.* Watertown,
MA: Charlesbridge Publishing, 2013.

Robert, Clyde Bulla. *The Story of Valentine's Day.*
New York: Harper Collins, 2000.

Ross, Kathy. *All New Crafts for Valentine's Day.*
Nashville, TN: 21st Century, 2002.

ON THE WEB

Visit our Web site for links about Valentine's
Day Crafts: **childsworld.com/links**

Note to Parents, Teachers, and Librarians:
We routinely verify our Web links to make sure they are safe and active
sites. So encourage your readers to check them out!

Index